REALITY OR RELIGION

JOSEPH R. CASTILLO

SENIOR PASTOR

Edition
First Edition: 2017

ISBN 978-132-6-94579-4

Publisher
Lulu.com

Published
February 16, 2017

Language
English

Contents

PREFACE

Congratulations!

This book that you are holding in your hand right now is by divine appointment. Things that affect our destiny never happen by accident because there is a God who loves us and desires to do a marvelous work in our lives. In order to ensure that you have the proper tools needed to have an abundant life of faith in Christ, I've prepared a short explanation of how God's plan for us has unfolded throughout history.

I would like you to see the word "History" in two parts. The first part is "His" and second part is " Story." When you look at world history, you're actually looking at the unfolding of God's plan for all creation. The amazing thing about the Bible is that you not only discover the past, and realize the present, but you also get a glimpse into the future. Your heavenly Father has already begun a good work in you, and this book will uncover the secret to winning in life.

In this book we will look at some important questions for our generation such as:

Does science and the Bible contradict itself?

Are you really not a "church" kind of person?

How to get God involved your my situation.

You will also discover:

1. What religion forgot about God.

2. How to have a down to earth heavenly experience

Chapter 1

History of the Universe

"God is the Father of all science, and the mystery of all creation lies in His perfection"

Planet Earth and the cosmos are billions of years old according to science. Most secular scientists agree on that, even some early Church writings including Jewish historians date the earth as such. However not only do both Jews and Christian scholars alike, agree that mankind as we know it has only been on earth for about 6,000 years.

Science also indicates such population growth in anthropological studies. History itself also gives overwhelming proof to support this fact.

Time, space and matter are in
continuum and need to come
into existence simultaneously. If there
was matter but no space, where would
you put it? If you have matter, and
space, but no time, when would you
put it? In addition to that, time has
past, present, and future; space
has length, width, height; and matter
has solid liquid gas, a trinity of trinities.

This is why we can't ask where God
came from, because that assumes He is
limited by time, space and matter. The
God who created time space and
matter did so from without
the limitations of such elements.

The first verse of the Bible states the
following:

"In the beginning (time) God created
the heavens (space) and the earth
(matter)." Genesis 1:1-2

Lets look at the next verse.

"And the earth was without form, and void; and darkness was upon the face of the deep. And the Spirit of God moved upon the face of the waters."

Now ask yourself what just happened there?

What could have happened between verse 1 and 2.

When the earth was made, it was made perfect, it was made to be inhabited.

"For thus saith the LORD that created the heavens (space); God himself that formed the earth (matter) and made it; he hath established it, he created it not in vain, he formed it to be inhabited" Isaiah 45:18

This word "vain" in Isaiah actually translates "without form or void". So if

God made the earth "with form", and it was not "void." Then what in the world could've happened in verse 2, when the earth was formless, void and uninhabitable?

Earth was an uninhabitable ball of ice, which some have called it an "Ice Age" of destruction and darkness. The earth was covered in water (maybe by a flood). We know there was no heating agent at this time, because the sun was not radiating light on earth until Genesis 1:3 and afterwards. So there we have it!

A completely flooded planet with no sunlight, perfectly explains the Ice Age. What could have happened after creation? Who and what lived on earth? How many seconds, hours, years or centuries had gone by before the earth was found in total destruction. What kind of animals or homo genus existed before Genesis 1:2? It's not clear if you don't understand eternity past.

There is a lot of research and science dealing with these subjects but what we know now is that Homo sapiens began with Adam in Genesis 1:26.

Perhaps between Genesis 1:1 and 1:2 the rebellion and fall of Lucifer (Satan the devil) took place. We know that Jesus said that, Lucifer rebelled against God and was cast out of heaven like lightning (Luke 10:18), but when did this occur?

From Adam's time in Genesis 1:26 even in till now, we have not seen any event like this in history, as a matter of fact Job tells us of a time in world history when Homo sapiens were not around to witness or record.

This galactic war that devastated the earth most likely happened in the period between Genesis 1:1 and 1:2. Science is not clear as to what actually caused the Ice Age. They're not clear as to the missing link between Homo sapiens as we know them today and the various species of homo genus fossils that lived millions of years ago. They're not certain as to how all the dinosaurs became extinct. Yet when we examine science through the microscope of God's word, it all becomes clear.

We know that the oldest recorded civilizations in the world are in the Middle East, China and Africa. Each of those civilizations only has documentation as far back as about 6,000 years ago, just like the Word of God describes. Those who read the Bible have a very accurate insight to what happened prior to Adam's creation found in the first few versus of Genesis.

I think it's very important for all Christians to really understand this, because what is called "Old Earth" is biblically supported, and taught by the some of the early Church fathers. It's also important because in the day that we live, science attempts to question the Word of God, and challenge faith in general.

If we presuppose a young earth and assume the planet is only 6,000 years old, just because Adam was, we instantly become unreasonable to the educated world. This isn't acceptable, since our God is the Father of all science, and the mystery of all creation lies in His perfection. In my 20 years of walking with God, I have never had an atheist or agnostic dismiss Christianity after taking them through the dozens of scriptures that point to an Old Earth, Ice Age and restoration of the Planet Earth.

The Bible is the oldest book in the world, and has been both the scientific and historical standard for centuries. The book of Job in particular is the oldest book of the world. In 30 BC a Roman engineer by the name of Marcus Vitruvius discovered the hydraulic cycle of precipitation, but that was 1,600 years after the Bible taught us the hydraulic cycle of precipitation in Job 36:27-28, Eccl 1:6-7; 11:3; Job 26:8; and Amos 9:6. Isn't the Word of God such an amazing source for science?

Though science once taught the earth was flat, the Bible taught that the earth was round (Isaiah 40:21-22). These are just two quick examples of God's word being scientifically precise, even when it was in direct opposition to what the world's leading scientist believed at that time, until science finally caught up and confirmed God's Word.

Now that we have briefly covered the creation of the universe, dinosaurs, global destruction and the restoration of planet Earth, lets do a quick over view of the history of humanity!

I hope to answer some very important questions like: Where did we come from? How did people end up all over the world? Why do we need salvation? Why are there so many different religions? How do we know Jesus Christ is Lord? Why did God have to send His son?

Chapter 2

History of Man

"Faith is not man made"

When God made Adam and Eve he called them both Adam, meaning "from the earth." He took dirt and formed the man's body. However man is much more than just dirt. Man's spirit came from the Father of all spirits directly when God breathed into Adam the breath of life and he became a living soul. Then God put Adam into a deep sleep and took from Adam's side, and fashioned the woman. Adam named her "Eve" because she was to be the mother of everyone who lived. After their creation God gave them both dominion over the whole earth.

Since that day God has never revoked their right to rule the earth and its affairs. Hid deeply inside the first few pages of the Bible we see the reasons for all human-inspired disaster, calamity, and violation that takes place in the world. Since all these terrible things were in the realm of human dominion and it' man who was fully responsible for; war, hunger, human trafficking, abuse, murder and even sickness cannot be blamed on God. Man made all these mistakes under the influence of the enemy. God is a good God, but He placed the affairs of this world under man's ultimate authority from the day they were created even until now.

The first thing that God did when he made man was to give him work. That's why the Bible says that if a man does not work he should not eat (2 Thessalonians 3:10).

He commanded them to replenish the earth, which means to "fill it again" suggesting the probable existence of a formerly populated earth prior to Genesis 1:2.

One of the most important things I want you to understand is this:

The first people to walk this planet knew who God was and worshipped Him. There was no question who was the most high God, creator of heaven and earth.

So contrary to popular belief, Faith is not "man made." People often say religion is man made, but not so.

God made religion. All throughout scripture you see God's engaging relationship with man, even after their fall. He told them to make altars, a temple, get priests, gather, pray and make sacrifices. The first people worshiped and served God. Religion is not merely a political strategy to "control the masses" as some foolish, intellectuals have said.

Sure, people might have used religion in the past to manipulate and control others. But the concept of pure religion, selfless, and sacred, comes from the one true God. And God, creator of heaven and earth, did not make several religions. He is one, and there is only one-way to worship one God and that's His way. He says in Acts 4:12 that there is only one name given to mankind from heaven where we can be saved by, and that's the name of Jesus.

Adam heard the voice of God who would walk with him in the cool afternoon breeze (Genesis 3:8). Human relationship with God continued in the garden until Adam sinned by eating from the Tree of the Knowledge of Good and Evil, which God had placed in the middle of the garden. When he ate of that tree Adam fell from perfection into a cycle of sin and death. Sin had entered Adam, and with it sickness of the spirit, soul and body, thus he became a living dead man.

When Adam and Eve began to have children, they were also born into the same state of spiritual death, because Adam was the capital head of all mankind. From Adam and Eve's disobedience, death was transferred to all mankind.

Even though Adam was now spiritually dead, he continued to walk with God. We know this from the account of his sons. Cain brought some of his fruit from the orchards, but his brother Abel brought a sacrifice that pleased God.

Abel's offering was favored because it was the first fruits the best of Abel's livestock. Giving our first fruits is God's way. When Cain saw that God had favored Abel's sacrificial giving he became jealous, flew into a rage and committed the first murder known to mankind. He killed his brother and as a result was sent away as a murderer.

This began a generation of people from Cain's bloodline that strayed away from God and into occult practice, witchcraft, and animism. This was the birth of false religion and its offshoots resulted in so many various belief systems as we have today.

Because Cain's descendants were not in right standing with God, they turned to other sources of spiritual power. Thus we can say confidently man made all "other" religions.

We live in a world where there's not only God and His Angels, but there are also evil spirits and demonic powers under Satan's control. Cain's line understood supernatural power and without a right standing relationship with God, they naturally turned to the power of the dark side to get ahead in life.

Adam and his wife had another boy by the name of Seth. In contrast to Cain, Seth's line continued to worship God. Eventually as the years went on, there were two kinds of people in the earth. Those who worshipped God and those who despised Him. Yet through all these ups and downs, both sides still remembered where they came from.

As time passed by, one of the wicked descendants of Cain became a powerful man of political stature. The leaders of his city began a building project involving the principles of occult art and intended to reach demonic powers in the heavenly realms. They conspired to contend with God's plan of redemption for mankind.

The fallen angels we read about in Genesis chapter 6 are also called "Watchers." They were the beings credited for giving advanced mathematical and scientific knowledge to the ancient Egyptians and Mayans.

Through the guidance of fallen angels (watchers) they were able to accomplish things and God Himself said, "nothing will be restrained from them, which they have imagined to do" (Genesis 11:6) in light of their unity of heart and mind.

Amazing things can be accomplished in unity, with or without God's present approval, because the blessing had already been given to us as chronicled in Genesis 1:26-28.

Actually much of the Greek mythology of gods coming down from heaven and having children with mankind comes from real accounts of the Watchers doing just that.

Some Egyptian hieroglyphs depict chariots coming down from heaven and having a leadership role among men, even teaching advanced angelic technology. Once again the Bible is giving us answers to things that have confused historians for years.

Modern day people think the chariots coming down to earth in the hieroglyphs were aliens. People think Stonehenge and the Mayan Pyramids are a mystery, but the Bible tells us exactly who these beings were and what they were doing in the earth.

When we get to Genesis chapter 11, everyone on earth is pretty much in the same general area of the planet. Since the time of Noah and his three sons (triplets) there were different colors of people.

The earth was full of wickedness, and the people of that day would not be deterred, working in perfect unity and filled with unimaginable evils. Someone was praying and asking God to stop the enemy, and God responded powerfully by dividing their languages and scattered them throughout the earth.

For century's secular anthropologists have been speculating about how the Native Americans ended up in the Americas and how the Chinese ended up in China and so forth. The answer is much simpler, precise, and astounding than supposed. God confused their language and transported them around the world from Babel. That's why to this day we call gibberish, babel.

This intervention of God had to be brought about through prayer. When people pray, they yield their God given authority back to the Father so He can begin to move in the earth. The Bible says that God does nothing in this earth without first revealing it to His servants the prophets (Amos 3:7).

The process looks something like this:

1. God reveals a need to us.

2. We pray in response to that need and stand in the gap asking for His will to be done on earth as it is in heaven.

3. God is released to intervene on our behalf.

Amen, that's exciting news. If you believe that, then say it loud, "Jesus, I release you into my problem!"

If you said that, I agree with you. Let a mighty wave of the intervention of Almighty God be released into your life in Jesus name!

God says something really interesting in the book of Ezekiel, "I sought for a man among them, that would stand in the gap, and make up the hedge for the land so it would not be destroyed, but I found none." Ezekiel 22:30

So God could not intervene to save, preserve and bless because no one was willing to stand up and pray on another one's behalf. The idea of making up a hedge is the concept of stepping in on the behalf of another, to defend them.

From the Tower of Babel account we understand how all races and tongues of the world have similar origins and how they arrived into their lands. Now that we know what happened, it shows us how it was possible for each ancient civilization to know about the reality of God.

They knew about the demonic realm such as dragons, snakes and spirits. (though their ancestors have been misled by these spirits and now believe that they can help them in some way). Each ancient civilization has a catastrophic flood account in their history. Most have understood and practiced the same processes of animal sacrifice in their early years of civilization.

Some have even built similar pyramids and altars of sacrifice without having ever met each other (at least not since their forefathers were in the city Babel together).

For example, ancient China has a narrative of early history from the Creation account to the Tower of Babel. That's even hidden in the characters of the Chinese language covering history as recorded in the Bible from Genesis chapter 1 all the way through chapter 11. Despite the amazing fact that a Christian Bible was not brought to China till thousands of years later.

They tell about the two people (Adam and Eve) made from the dust of the ground in the garden.

園 ＝ 土 ＋ 口 ＋ 囗 ＋ 亻 ＋ 人
garden　dust　breathe　house　person　people

造 ＝ 辶 ＋ 告 （ 丿 ＋ 土 ＋ 口 ）
create　walk　talk　living　dust　mouth (people)

洪＝氵＋共（卄＋一＋八）
flood　water　total　together　earth　eight

船＝舟＋八＋口
boat　vessel　eight　mouth (people)

We learn about the fall of man with the serpent in a tree, and even about the total earth being flooded and the 8 people (Noah and his family) who survived by building a in a vessel. It's all in ancient Chinese literature and characters!

The earth has never been void of the knowledge of the One, True God. Early followers of God called Him various names or titles, but all those are ascribed to the same creator of heaven and earth. For example God revealed himself to Moses as "I am." For thousands of years people were afraid to speak or even write His name. Often times they would just call Him the LORD. This tradition is still followed today by the Jewish people, many will write G-d instead of GOD. In ancient times they would write YHVH, an abbreviation of Yahweh, taking out the vowels because His name was considered too sacred to speak. Yet the knowledge of God has been here from the first man till this day.

CHAPTER 3

KEEPING THE BLOODLINE PURE

Everything starts with God. His plan of salvation for mankind was to come through the womb of a woman. Right in the beginning of the Bible when Adam and Eve sinned God revealed his plan by saying the woman shall bear a child and this child shall crush Satan's head. So now the enemy's counterattack was to corrupt the bloodline.

Gods people had to maintain a pure bloodline going all the way back to Adam. So God chose someone from

Adam and Eves bloodline to teach their children His ways and keep not only their bloodline pure, but also protect the faith till the prophesied Christ would come to crush Satan's head.

So God chose Abram from Ur of the Chaldeans. The language of his people was Hebrew, the oldest language in the world and believed by many to be the language God used to create the universe. The word Hebrew comes from one of the Hebrew's forefather, Eber in Genesis 10. Who according to Rabbinical tradition didn't participate in the building of the tower of Babel.

God spoke to Abram and his wife Sara and tells them they are going to have a son, and that this promised son will give birth to a mighty nation of people and all families of the earth will be blessed by his offspring. This was a prophecy that God's Christ would come from their bloodline.

But the problem was that Abram was old, and Sara was old, in fact she was beyond childbearing age. So they took things into their own hands and Abram went into another woman by the name of Hagar and had Ishmael. But this seed had to be from Abram and Sara.

There may have been a bloodline issue that Abram didn't understand, so God revisits Abram and renames him Abraham which means "Father of a multitude" and admonishes him saying, this promise seed must come from Sarah's womb, the pure bloodline to give birth to Isaac.

In the fullness of time Abraham and Sarah give birth to Isaac. Isaac goes on to have some children and the blessing is transferred down to his son Jacob.

God changes Jacob's name to "Israel"
and Israel goes on to have 12 sons who
will become the historical 12 tribes of
Israel. Joseph was not one of the tribes
because his offspring took that role
in lieu of him, because he ended up
in Egypt, and became a prime minister,
CEO under the Pharaoh.

When famine came to the land, Israel
and his other 11 sons joined Joseph in
Egypt and as years passed by Joseph
dies and the Egyptian government
enslaves the Jewish people. God's new
nation, "Israel" ends up in slavery for
400 years.

The more the Egyptian government
told them to stop reproducing, the
more children were born to them, and
the more they were persecuted the
mightier they became, the more they
were afflicted the more they multiplied.
In time their cries reach God and He

rose up a Hebrew man who grew up in Pharaohs royal court by the name of Moses. God uses Moses to deliver them out of slavery and bring them into the land of Canaan. This land was the place that God had promised to Abraham and his descendants a long time ago, but forewarned him that they would have to go through 400 years of slavery.

After a series of miracles Israel becomes a mighty nation and would later become the breeding ground of some of the mightiest kings in world history including the famous King David and the wisest man to ever live - King Solomon. Throughout the generations God continued to preserve His people through the law and the prophets commitment to religious devotion. This unchanging religion began with God from the first man Adam, from Adam to Abraham

and from Abraham all the way to Mary
and Joseph thousands of years later
until the Roman Empire occupied the
land of Israel.

O JERUSALEM I WILL NOT FORGET YOU

Many things happened around the
world, other religions such as
Hinduism and Buddhism came out of
India. In fact Asia has been called the
cradle for all major world religions
since Adam.

Through the centuries from Adam till
Christ, God's people were merely
trying to survive in the land of Israel,
and in their ancient capital city of
Jerusalem peacefully awaiting the
Messiah, but it was not as peaceful as
they hoped. Not one city in world
history has survived so much; though
Israel is one of the oldest countries in

the world, paradoxically, it's also one of the youngest. It's the only country to have been reborn out of antiquity and be revived again after a struggle just as dramatic as any struggle ever recorded in the Old Testament.

The Jews are the only people to have been scattered throughout the world, bitterly persecuted for over 2,000 years, yet gathered together into a nation again. Israel's language (Hebrew) is the only speech to have been resurrected from a dead language, to a living, virile, and modern one.

Israel exists on a strip of land so narrow that on most maps its name must be printed outside its borders, yet it possesses more historic and sacred sites to mankind than any other country in the world.

Today compressed into those narrow borders is a microcosm of the world, for the average Israeli, his or her parents, have migrated from any of more than one hundred different lands. To live in Israel today is like living in a pressure-cooker always under tension.

From the second day of their restoration they have been under constant attack from their neighbors, out numbering them in the millions, yet the Israel continues to expand and develop more rapidly than larger countries around the world.

The revival of Israel in the Holy Land today is the beginning of the restoration of everything spoken of by the prophets for centuries, and as we watch in the days ahead we will see that the Holy Land becomes greater and greater in global significance. The City of Peace has been fought for over sixteen times, destroyed twice, besieged 23 times, attacked 52 times, and captured or recaptured 44 times. Israel is a nation where God has placed His name, and the miraculous has been normal for thousands of years!

CHAPTER 4

FULLNESS OF TIME

"SHE'S FAR FROM PERFECT BECAUSE
SHE'S HUMAN, YET SHE CAN'T BE
STOPPED BECAUSE SHE'S ALSO DIVINE"

When the fullness of time had come,
the world had various religions, maybe
millions of "man made" religious
beliefs and superstitions. Yet there
remained a nation of people around the
world who had not yet ceased to
worship Moses's "I Am" and Adams'
"Voice Walking in the Cool of the
Day."

People were still following Abel's God,
the God of Sarah's miracle baby, and
their bloodline remained undefiled
from the 5th century BC to around the
1st Century AD when Christ was born.

A young teenage girl by the name of Mariam (Mary) appears on the scene. She gets a visit from the Angel Gabriel in the same manner her early ancestor Sarah was visited. But this time the message was a little bit different because Mariam was a virgin. Sarah said: "how can this be? I'm old!" but Mariam said "how can this be, I'm a virgin!" It's pretty normal for people to ask how can this kind of question when they have a divine encounter.

Jesus, the only begotten son of God, conceived in the womb of a virgin in the fullness of time, had laid all His Godhead ability aside and humbled himself as a human baby, and grew to become the sacrificial lamb who would take away the sin of the world.

He gave his life as a sacrifice for our sin; he was the only one who could, because Adam was a perfect man. No one after Adam could qualify as a sacrifice because everyone born from Adam's loins were the unrighteous offspring of a spiritually dead man, they couldn't qualify as a perfect sacrifice.

Jesus Christ, God the Son, born of a virgin, pure in His blood and in His linage, the prophesied seed of Abraham who would crush Satan's head had come. Perfect in all His ways with undefiled blood, He became the sacrifice to balance the scales of justice.

He who had never sinned became sin for us, so we can be made righteous. When he rose from the dead three days later and defeated death, He breathed into us the Breath of Life again and we became Born Again, from death to life. Now we are living souls once again. The life of God living on the inside of us, born into His Kingdom.

AGE OF THE CHURCH

After Christ died for the sins of mankind, and He defeated death, hell and the grave by resurrection from the dead, He then took His perfect blood into heaven and offered it as a perfect sacrifice for the forgiveness of our sins, after doing so he sent Holy Spirit to fill and empower His newborn children.

For a few hundred years this newborn body of believers turned the world upside down by performing miracles, raising the dead. They were used in extraordinary signs and wonders while simultaneously under persecution.

The more they were told not to preach the more the church grew, the more they were persecuted the mightier they became, the more they were afflicted the more they multiplied. During this same period countless people were stoned, fed to lions, burned alive and tortured for their testimony of Jesus Christ. But it didn't slow down the Church growth one bit. It spread all over the known world and into the Far East, some say as far as Korea.

Finally after a couple centuries of persecution, the Church won. The Emperor of Rome by the name of Constantine converted to Christianity. The gospel of Christ perhaps had reached the most powerful man on earth at that time.

He gathered as many Christians as he could and established the Eastern Capital for Constantinople.

During this time government control and the institutionalization of the Church began, and with it a dark age for the Church. Political leaders became religious leaders, many with no fear of God and without a genuine relationship with God, began to rule the people of God with man-made unbiblical teachings and extra-religious rules and rites.

Schisms and divisions began to take place and this government was divided into Eastern Orthodoxy and Western Catholicism. I'd like to note here that there remained an independent Ethiopian Church, Egyptian Church and a far Eastern Church as well during all these events.

Eventually normal people could not even read the Bible which led to much more Church abuse. Further reformation came into the Roman Catholic Church, led by a German priest by the name Martin Luther.

This was known as the Protestant Reformation, originating from the word to protest. Many people in the world today are under the false presumption that Christians are either Catholic, Protestant or Orthodox, but there are many Churches that are before these two entities or outside of them.

Not only are there Churches as old as the Catholic and
Orthodox Churches there are also people who have come to Christ and practice their faith and have not affiliation with Orthodox, Catholic, and Ethiopian. For example, a Muslim has a vision of Jesus Christ and is born again; he/she is neither Catholic nor protestant, but just a Christian until he decides to join a local congregation.

Yet in the Roman Catholic Church as well as various other streams of Christianity that flowed through the world from the time of Christ's first disciples till now, there have been many great people of devout faith. Even during the peak of the Roman Churches apostasy, there were still hundreds of thousands of both genuine and devout Catholics, both lay and clergy, whose hearts were near to the heart of Christ.

Even though much of the Church was political and far removed from the truth of God's word, there were great men and women of God within their ranks.

There have been many priests, bishops and saints in both the Catholic, Orthodox, Eastern, Egyptian, and Ethiopian Churches who were mighty men and women of God. They knew Him in an intimate way, walked with God and in His glory during the hardest times of Church history.

During these dark ages many diabolical sects and religions formed. Islam was born and many other deviations from the true religion of YHWH (The, "I Am"). Yet from Adams first breath till today, there has never been a moment on earth where people didn't call upon the name of the Lord.

Christ's Church now numbers about one third of the people on the planet, and Christianity is the world's largest religion. Christianity is the only religion that demonstrates miraculous power, and when encountering demonic manifestations of those possessed in "man made" religions, the power of the Holy Spirit, in Jesus name, always makes an open defeat and show of the devil.

The Christian Church is the only entity on earth that can prove other religions wrong by a visible demonstration of

God's power. The Christian Church also contains the world's most accurate and detailed genealogy from Adam till now.

The Judeo-Christians possesses the oldest and most original manuscripts in world history "The Holy Bible." The Christian Church has more universities, kindergartens, high schools, colleges, hospitals, orphanages and homes for the homeless than any other religious or secular entity in the history of the planet.

The Christian Church is the true body of God's Kingdom in the earth. This Church is not only His embodiment on the earth, but also lovingly known as His bride and He is coming back for His bride very soon. Oh, but she's far from perfect because she's human, yet she can't be stopped because she's also divine.

Chapter 5

Repent and be Baptized

"God's will for your life is not only that you fully follow Him, but that you be fully filled by Him"

I was born again out of a lifestyle of addiction and substance abuse. One of the things that God used to help me was NA (Narcotics Anonymous-12 step recovery from addiction program). In NA and also in AA (Alcoholics Anonymous-12 step recovery from addiction program) and so on, they always said to us, "your best way of doing things has got you this far."

If you want to create a new future for your life, you must fully surrender to God's way of doing things. The word for being "Fully Surrendered" to God can be called, repentance.

Repent comes from a Greek military term that means "about face." In other words "take a 180 degree turn away from your way of doing things, and become fully reliant on God." When Jesus said "repent for the Kingdom of God is at hand" (Mark 1:15), He was saying turn away from your way of doing things, because God's way has arrived! In another place He said, "I am the Way, the Truth and the Life, no man comes to the Father but by me" (John 14:6).

Our Lord Jesus Christ is the only way into the Kingdom of God. But for many people when we hear the term "Kingdom of God" they may imagine a former church experience, or a movie they once saw.

But to get a proper perspective we need to look past our old ideas of religion and only focus on what God's Word says in order to get a true definition and concept of what His Kingdom is.

Sometimes the best way to describe a thing is to simply say what it's not, and when God described the Kingdom, that's how He approached it, saying "The Kingdom of God is NOT meat or drink, but righteousness peace and joy in the Holy Ghost" (Romans 14:17). I'd like to add to that, and tell you that the Kingdom of God is not a church, a race, or any particular culture. However in Gods kingdom there are many races of people, various cultures, church styles, and different Christian denominations.

Once you have the King of the Kingdom living in your heart by the Holy Spirit, this kingdom is no longer at hand, but actually on the inside of you. It's not confined to a geographical place, but it's more like any colonial power. The Kingdom of God is wherever the rule of the King extends.

So we find that in many churches there may be some aspects of God's Kingdom and at the same time, you could experience aspects of mans culture or style. For example, we may see joy, love and peace in a church; these are all fruits of God's kingdom, yet the music may vary.

It could be modern music or may be old-fashioned. The style of music is according to the church leaders' preference not necessarily God's. After all, God made all nations, tribes and tongues, I'm sure God loves variety.

One style or method of worship is neither right nor wrong, but a simple expression of how we show our love to the Lord. Meanwhile the presence of God may be there, as His expression of the Kingdom among us.

Welcome to the Kingdom!

Once you repent and turn to God you now belong to an international, interstellar body of believers from various Christian denominations, nations, and expressions of faith in Jesus Christ not only on this earth but also in heaven.

Since you have repented and put your life in Jesus' hands, you have become a new person in Him (2 Corinthians 5:17). The old sinful nature you had died, and you have a new life. This is a literal New Birth of your spirit man.

Now it's time to get water baptized. This is not something we should wait on. Why?

Baptism means to be dunked or fully submerged under water. It's an act of obedience to God.
Being submerged under water in the likeness of Christ's death, burial, and resurrection. When you go under the water it's a burial of your old man. When you come out of the water, it's your resurrection, just like Christ was resurrected out of the grave; you are resurrected to your new life!

This is the first test of true repentance; it shows everyone in heaven and earth that you are obedient to God, even as Christ was obedient to the Father for your sake, and laid down his life for you.

Baptism is a command, not a suggestion. Even Jesus himself went to be baptized. We can easily argue Why did "God the Son" need to be baptized!?

He created the water for heaven sakes!

Well, we aren't the only ones to feel that way. When Jesus went to be baptized; he was questioned by the prophet called "John the Baptist" who said, "I should be baptized by you."

But Jesus replied "it's necessary for me to fulfill the law" (Matthew 3:14-15). Baptism is necessary; it's the second part of the process. In the old covenant God commanded the priests on the Day of Atonement to take two goats, identical one to another.

The priest would cast lots and the goat that the lot fell on was given to the Lord as a sacrifice to cover sin. But that was not enough. The sins of the people can be removed, so they would lay hands on the scapegoat and he would be sent away, representing the sending away of their sins. The first goat died to cover their sins; the second was sent away.

In like manner the first step is believing in your heart and confessing with your mouth the Lord Jesus. When you do that you are born again and your sins are forgiven.

The second step is an outward act of obedience where your sins are sent away through baptism (Acts 2:38). Therefore you must be baptized in the name of Jesus Christ for the sending away of your sins, soon after you repent and believe. Both are to be done at the same time, that is if you have water nearby.

It's nice to be baptized in a Church, but any pool, river, lake or even a horse trough will do! My Pastor Dr. Bill Winston in Chicago, used to use a horse trough in the kitchen of a nightclub to baptize new believers each Sunday immediately after the call for salvation.

HOLY SPIRIT BAPTISM

Holy Spirit is God, that's why I don't even use the word "the" too often when referencing Him. He is a person, just as much as Abba Father and Jesus Christ. These three distinct beings are one. I know it's not easy for humans to wrap our minds around divinity, but an easy way to explain the triune nature of God is to look at yourself.

In Genesis God made man in His image and in His likeness. He made you spirit, soul and body. You are a spirit, you live in a body, and you possess a soul. Your soul is where the mind, will, and emotions operate. Your spirit, soul and body are all 100% you.

You are not three separate people. Yet each part of you, has a separate critical function that when brought altogether makes you ONE complete person made in His image, and in His likeness.

The Godhead is 3 in one:
Father, Son and Holy Spirit.

Humans are 3 in one: Spirit, Soul and body. Soul can be defined as: mind, heart, will, and emotions:

1. Father (Our Soul)

2. Son (Our Body)

3. Holy Spirit (Our Spirit)

Now that we have been:

1. Born again (which affects our spirit man)

2. Water baptized (which affects our bodily man)

There is another crucial step in our conversion experience.

3. Baptism in the Holy Spirit (which affects our soul man) *how the body reacts to the power of God baptizing your soul varies*

The baptism of the Holy Spirit is the infusing of God's power in our soul. The Holy Spirit is already in our spirit man when we became born again. But our Christian life will be processed through our soul. The salvation of God will manifest in our natural life to the degree it flows out of our soul.

Our soul is the middle ground between our spirit (where Holy Spirit is) and the physical world where our body will walk in victory or defeat.

Since our soul life is the determining factor to Christ's salvation being manifested in and through our lives, He said he would send this with a miraculous manifestation upon its arrival. It is essential to have this baptism of the Holy Spirit.

Now that we have experienced step 1 and 2, step 3 is a consummating step in radical God-like transformation. This is so important that Jesus commanded the Church saying, "don't go anywhere till you get the power."

There are several baptisms in scripture, the first one is in water, the second one is this Luke 24:49 baptism where He said "Tarry ye in the city of Jerusalem, until you be endued with power from on high."

John the Baptist prophesied about this baptism of power from on high saying "I baptize you with water (our body), but some one is coming greater than me, and he shall baptize you with the Holy Ghost and Fire (our soul)." Matthew 3:11

In the beginning of this book I spoke about being wholly surrendered to God. This means doing all that Jesus said. That means you should love your neighbor, pray for those who are spiteful, also wait for the promised baptism of the Holy Spirit.

So many people ask Jesus to forgive their sins, but they never actually repented and followed Christ all the way to the cross in death. That means following God even to the place of sacrificing our own ideas and opinions. There is a famous fast food chain from America called Burger King, and their motto is "Your way, right away."

However that's not how the Kingdom of God works. It's His Kingdom, He is the King, and it's His way. God's will for your life is not only that you fully follow Him, but also that you be fully filled by Him.

That's why the word "baptism" is used of the Holy Spirit, just like being fully dunked in water. Jesus wants you to be fully soaked in Him.

Have you ever bought a new car and tried to drive it home with no fuel? The fact is that beautiful car, with all the comforts and benefits of air conditioning, heated seats, mp3 player, sunroof and so on, will never be fully enjoyed if it has no fuel to power it.

You need God, to live for God. In other words you need the Holy Spirit to live for Jesus.

Jesus said it like this to His disciples. I'm going away, but "I'm going to send another Comforter, He's going to be in you and with you." John 14:16; 16:5-7

We can't cut corners and take short cuts when we are coming to Christ; we can't overlook obedience by rejecting the steps of water baptism or the baptism of the Holy Ghost.

How do you get baptized in the Holy Ghost? Simply ask! Matthew 7:7 says "whosoever asks, shall receive." So get in a prayer position most comfortable for you, lift up you hands, close your eyes and focus on Gods presence because He is there with you right now! Next step, just ask!

God only requires 2 things when you ask.

1. Believe that He is real (Hebrews 11:6).

2. Believe you receive while you're praying (Mark 11:24).

Now you're alone, you're quite, you're in a comfortable prayer posture; your hands are lifted high.

Simply ask Jesus to forgive you of your sins (believe it and receive it in your heart). Then ask Him to fill you with His Holy Spirit (believe that, and receive that too in your heart).

Next, open your mouth in praise; you can simply praise Him by repeatedly saying "Hallelujah."

You may do so until you begin to speak in another language or a stuttering comes over your words. Within a short time you will be speaking in a heavenly language that you never learned before. This language is an initial evidence of you being baptized in the Holy Ghost.

Here is an example prayer:

"Father I come to you know in Jesus name, I ask you to forgive me of my sin, wash me in your blood.

I reject all witchcraft and occultism and I declare Jesus Christ as my Lord.

Now Lord Jesus, I ask you, to baptize me now with the Holy Spirit and fire, I believe it with my heart and confess it with my mouth.

Give me the gift of praying in unknown tongues and fill me with power from on high. In Jesus name, amen!"

Now you got it.

Repentance, Baptism with water and the Holy Spirit can happen all in one day. You're born again, baptized in water and filled with the Holy Spirit and well on your way to the greatest days of your life.

CHAPTER 6

CHURCH KIND OF PERSON

"GOD'S ORIGINAL PURPOSE FOR
PLACING A PASTOR IN THE CHURCH IS
TO BOTH PROTECT AND FEED THE
SHEEP"

You have your whole life ahead of you,
it's important to allow your recent
experience to become a major
stepping-stone into a lifetime of joy,
peace, blessings, and prosperity.

The Hebrew language consolidates all
these things into one word, "shalom."
In order to do this you must cultivate
your spiritual life. Like a tender young
plant you need sunshine, water and
love.

Without being connected to good soil,
the plant may soon whither. To avoid

this you must join a healthy church, read the Bible daily and pray. Prayer simply means talking with God, it's a two-way conversation.

The fourth step in your journey is finding the best church body that you can. For some people that means a 2 to 4 hour commute each week. For others it's only a 5 minute walk, either way get to the closest Church you can find, attend all the services your work schedule permits, and lay down roots there!

Find a Bible preaching Christian church. Avoid any large well-known cults like The Church of Jesus Christ of Latter-Day Saints (Mormons), Kingdom Hall (Jehovah Witnesses), The Unification Church (Moonies)! Preferably find a Full-Gospel Church that believes in the entirety of the Bible!

We can use the Bible as
our safety guideline while looking for a
church to join.

Mark 16: 17-18 lists the signs of those
who believe in His name.

1. Speak in new tongues

2. Cast out devils

3. Lay hands on the sick, and they
actually recover

4. Take up serpents (Satan and his
demons are the serpents)

5. Drink any deadly thing and will not
be harmed (supernatural health)

The Kingdom of God is a living body;
one part cannot function without the
other. You need to be nourished in the
word of God and meet other believers

for prayer, study and fellowship. This is how to strengthen your faith.

Often you'll find the richest and closest relationships in the family of God. Being fed a healthy spiritual diet of the Word of God requires a balance of Christian resources. I don't suggest listening to one minister only, but rather glean from the foundation of both ancient and proven modern-day Apostles, Prophets, Evangelists, Pastors and Teachers.

For a healthy diet you need personal Bible study, good Christian books by credible authors. Visit other churches, conferences or events outside of your local church's normal services times (with your pastor or leaders notification and blessing).

These activities can help you have a healthy spiritual diet as well as global

perspective of God's
kingdom. Beware of any
church that does not allow you to visit
other Churches and events, yet never
miss your Churches
main activities for another.

The pastor of your local church may be
a great teacher or prophet. But God
has given us Apostles, Prophets,
Pastors, Teachers, and Evangelists for
the perfecting of the saints, for the
work of the ministry.

If we only hear teaching in the area that
our local pastor is well studied or gifted
in, then we will lack in other areas he is
not so strong in. For example if a
pastor knows all about the end times
and Bible prophesy but very little about
the sanctification process of the Holy
Spirit, we will grow unbalanced.

On the other side of the coin if you don't submit under your own Church leadership long enough you'll never get your church's spiritual DNA, and will not have a solid foundation. The higher you want to grow in your spiritual life the deeper a foundation you need to lay.

Simply put, each credible Christian minister has a gift or grace upon his or her lives to bless the body of Christ in unique ways. With that said, being submitted to one local church gives you the safety net to protect you from false teaching and other pitfalls that you may encounter in your walk with the Lord.

A Christian cannot read a bunch of books, pray, attend a lot of different churches and expect to have a healthy spiritual life if they don't plant roots in ONE local church. Not being properly submitted to discipleship and accountability within that community is very dangerous for any believer.

God's original purpose for placing a pastor in the church is to protect, guide and feed the sheep. This responsibility is so serious that the Bible says that the pastor will give an account to God, on your behalf, for your soul. Your pastor will answer to God about you one day.

How serious is that!

But how can a pastor speak into your life if you're not a committed attendee? What can he say if you're always in and out? If we don't submit ourselves to the process of church discipleship we steal from our own development and potential. The word "disciple" means disciplined one; it comes from the Greek concept of a teacher and his pupil.
The disciples were to take

new believes under their wing and lead them through the disciplines of a Christian life. If you never fully submit to a church, you will never fully become a disciple of Christ. That inevitably leads to forming your own kind on unbiblical religious experience.

That being said we should only have one church membership, and one pastor. Support that church by attending regularly, donating offerings, paying your tithes and volunteering as part of your worship to God.

Does that mean that you must live and die in the first church you ever joined?

Not necessarily. Many people move to other places or countries and when they do so, they should join the local church in that area and transfer their membership.

They're may be a time in someone's life where God will call them to change churches within their own area. If that happens, you should first discuss and pray about it with your pastor and get a letter of recommendation in order to avoid being spiritually unruly or rebellious. You should never leave a church on bad terms, or to escape an uncomfortable situation that has arose. Never leave a church out of anger, bitterness, pride or resentment.

There is another type of people as well that come in the church and the Bible calls them goats. They may rebel, cause fights and division and are usually not submissive to authority. The pastor must love both, but Jesus will separate the goats from the sheep in his return. The sheep will go heaven and the goats will receive the judgment of God. In the case of a sin that one refuses to give up, the church may ask someone not to volunteer or not to attend the fellowship any longer. Especially if that sin is hurting others or causing others to fall into temptation too. Obviously people who indulge in sexual sin (i.e. pedophilia, seduction), thievery, sowing divisions or conflict may be asked not to attend the church if they have refused to provide evidence of repentance.

In these situations church discipline is totally necessary and may result in being put out and cut off from all fellowship.

While church leaders should speak into your life, "disciple" you, comfort you, correct you and so on, they should never lord over you. A pastor or a leader can and should give you godly counsel from His word, but at the end of the day, respect and love you even if your decisions are contrary to their

advice. If you feel that your pastor is abusive, controlling and
their teaching wrong in doctrine. There are several steps you can take according to the scriptures, which give you
a healthy way to help the pastor. By following God's way of handling things help to ensure you are also not hurt in the process and fall away disillusioned. God give you the grace to move on, when you have done it the right way. He wants you to move into the next season of your life in a healthy
and positive way, while maintaining peace with others.

It's easy to leave a church when you are frustrated or confused. Scenarios like this have happened since the beginning of time, and since every church is filled with people it will continue to happen. People are often referred to as sheep in the Bible, and sheep can be messy and problematic. We realize we are broken and in need of the love of God through Jesus Christ. This love that God gives us he also expects us to give back to others, to look past each other's faults and love one another unconditionally. This is why I said; you can find the richest relationships in the church, because we should love you unconditionally.

With that said, IT'S OKAY to change Churches. If God is leading you to do so, and you have peacefully and patiently attempted to get the blessing of your leadership, you may go forward in joy to the next level.

Often times another church means God is taking you to another level.

WORSHIP THROUGH GIVING

I mentioned earlier, as Christians we give our first fruits and offerings to our local Church as part of our worship. Tithe is a Bible word that means the first ten percent of our income.

Giving is the greatest universal expression of faith towards God. From the very beginning when God made man and placed him in the garden there was a tree given to man, but God asked man not to touch what He gave him.

This principle goes on throughout Scripture including Adam's children. Abel understood giving to God from the first part of his increase. Abel gave the first part of his flocks to God as a sacrifice of worship.

The great patriarchs of the faith continued in this example before God ever placed it in the Law. We see this with Abraham, when he met Melchizedek the high priest of God, he gave him tithes of all!

Later on we see how this act of worship and expression of great faith is connected to God's blessing in Malachi 3:10-12. Where God commands us to bring all the tithes into His house and promises to open the windows of heaven and pour us out a blessing we cannot contain.

In this part of the Bible God actually invites us to challenge Him and watch how He will rebuke Satan on our behalf. Later on in the New Testament the Bible teaches that even though we put our tithe into the hands of a human, that in reality it's going directly to Jesus Christ our Great High Priest! This is the only place God ever said we should test him.

An unbeliever can't tithe because it seems like they're just throwing money away. But for those who really know God, they realize we can't afford to miss our tithe because it's the greatest investment a person can make.

In most churches you cannot volunteer or be a leader if you are not a tither because God considers that an act of unbelief and ultimately robbery. Why robbery? Because all that we have comes from God and therefore God can ask us to give back 100% if He desires. But God allows us to keep 90% and return to Him 10% as an act of faith and in turn He promises to increase our 90%. Many in the church give much more than 10%. Some people have so raised their tithe that God has blessed them to live off the 10% and they give 90% away in donations.

Even my church gives over 10% of all our collection away. Simply because we trust God to keep His Word, and bless the church with an open heaven and pour us out a blessing that there is not room enough to contain it

SHARING LIFE WITH OTHERS

Perhaps the most exciting thing about your new joy and experience is sharing it with others. Actually I think there is no greater joy than leading others to Jesus Christ. There is an actual awesome experience of super natural joy that we experience when we lead others to Christ. It's awesome and addicting at the same time.

It's often an awkward thing to try and do, but once you start you can't stop. When people stop winning souls because they get busy with life and other stuff and quickly they begin to lose their fire. New life gives birth to life, and when a church is full of new life it duplicates and multiplies.

But when you work in the church it's easy to be so busy with church duties that you forget about the heartbeat of the Church, which is salvation of the lost! The Church is a "spiritual delivery room" so to speak, and we must maintain a level of excitement for each new baby born into faith in Christ.

I remember when I first got saved. The State of Illinois had declared me a menace to society and wanted to put me in the department of corrections. But my probation officer pleaded with the judge saying I had a bad upbringing and a bad life. "There is good in him if you would just give him a chance." She said.

The judge said "one last chance and we'll send him to a high security facility far away from Chicago so he can't runaway." No facilities in Illinois would accept me because of my criminal record so I had to go out of State. Only two places would take me; Eau Claire, Wisconsin and some other city in Nebraska. I figured if I escaped, Wisconsin is much closer to Chicago, so I chose Eau Claire. I was admitted as a resident at the Eau Claire Academy on 550 Dewy Street, in Eau Claire, Wisconsin.

It was the ice-cold winter of January 1996. I was released from 1100 S. Hamilton Correctional facility in Chicago and shipped off 7 hours north to Wisconsin, where the snow was taller than the cars on the highway.

It was getting close to Valentines Day and I was beginning to feel sad, empty and lonely. Because it was Valentines Day just one year ago that my mother told me she was dying of AIDS and that she had only three months left to live and the 1-year anniversary since that grisly night had arrived. On the bright side of things, I haven't seen ladies in a long time so I was happy to see that upon arrival there were not only boys but also girls.

I heard there was a chapel in the basement where you can meet girls so I want down there to see this girl I wanted to pass a note to.

That day a team of missionaries were in Wisconsin from Mexico. They didn't speak much English and I wasn't going to listen anyways but they performed a mime show of the crucifixion of Jesus Christ.

After their performance we were dismissed and many people left but me, I was waiting for my escort to take me back up to the evaluation unit so I was just stuck there with these missionaries.

A young girl named Amber and I.
While we waited the
missionaries shared with us, prayed for
us and "HOT DOG!"

I got saved!

I ran upstairs and shared my faith with
all my roommates at the time,
I can't remember what the other guys
all said but I had one Fish Head (a Fish
Head is a modern day Dead Head,
which is people who follow a particular
band around America doing drugs)
who really came against me.
He believed in aliens and said God was
not real.

I was so confident in the reality of God
at that time I offered him a deal. I said
if you commit to pray with me every
night for 1 month, and God does
not reveal himself to you, then I will
not believe in God either and I meant

it. I was kind of putting God on the line saying if you don't answer his prayers, for your glory then you will lose 2.

We prayed every night, he swore during his prayers, he said I'm wasting my time talking to floor. I was praying too, "Lord please don't reveal yourself by a lightening bolt on his head."

After about 3 weeks and a series of miracles in his life, his family and many signs and wonders he was on fire for God, worshipping, reading his Bible and praying without curse words anymore.

Before long we were evangelizing the whole unit, having Bible studies and me and my best friend Thomas Weir both left the Academy together and became roommates in Chicago, going to Church, serving God and preaching to everyone we met, everywhere we went. Evangelism is the lifeblood to our faith, when we lead others to Jesus we remember how we were once saved. I remember how far we have come and the fire keeps burning.

My life changed because somebody took the time to leave their country, spend thousands of dollars on flights, hotels and so on. Just so they can share Christ with us drug addict kids in a high security rehab facility in the middle of ice frozen Wisconsin. And thank God they did, there is no price too high, no distance too far, no inconvenience in life that not worth bringing a young boy like me to Jesus Christ.

I never met those guys again, but 20 years later I am thankful to them, and everyone who donated to send them to America. I'm thankful to the US consulate for giving those guys visa's and to the staff at Eau Claire Academy for not being so politically correct and allow missionaries to come and speak to us.

My only question is this. Why did God have to bring these guys from Mexico through all those hurdles in going to Wisconsin to reach me? The reason is clear sad to say, simply because the thousands of Christians, and hundreds of churches in the City of Eau Claire were just not doing it themselves.

Don't be the hindrance to another's salvation.

Proverbs 14: 5 says A true witness delivereth souls.

We must be a witness of the grace that we have received, and as we deliver souls we are bringing to God the one thing that He cares most about, and that is people. Brining His children back to Him, letting them know that he loves them so much, that he gave his life for them. Never let a month go by where you haven't personally led someone to Jesus Christ. They are ready, it's only the selfishness of Christians, that overshadows the potential harvest of new people coming to Christ.

CHAPTER 7

GOD SAVES A GANGSTER

"I CAN REMEMBER THOSE DAYS IN THAT ROACH AND MICE INFESTED APARTMENT"

I was born in the city of Chicago. Both of my parents were involved in the sales and use of drugs from before the time I was born. I wasn't even 3 years old when I had my first contact with the police, as they raided my house and arrested my father for illegal drug sales. By the time I was four years old, my mother and father had separated. My dad moved to Los Angeles to stay with his brother. There, he continued in illegal activity until shortly after he was shot and killed. My mom was engaged in various illegal activities as she continued to use and sell drugs until she remarried and gave birth to my little sister.

Now living with my stepfather, I became the victim of severe abuse. My stepfather was both physically and emotionally abusive. He would abuse me in horrific ways like cutting and burning. This continued until one day when my grandmother saw that my entire back and behind was black from a beating. Even though I was afraid for my life, she managed to get me to admit to her what had happened. My mother immediately divorced him, yet for some reason unknown to me, my little sister went with him, and I with our mom. Meanwhile, my older sister had long since been with my grandmother, due to my mom's inability to raise two children on her own. So now it was just my mom and I.

I can remember those days in that roach and mice infested apartment, they are forever seared in my conscious. In that time in my life there were so many bad memories like the many times I had to wipe the blood off my mother's brow after being beaten by her boyfriend. I will never forget the time I ran outside to the pay phone to call the police for help. Rather than helping, the police left us alone saying they were tired of coming over there for the same thing. Nor will I forget the time I had to give my mom a knife to stab the man trying to choke her to death.

It was in that same apartment I believe my mother contracted AIDS. One night my mom said she would be home by 10 and at 12am I was still waiting for her return by the window. This was just one of many times I was left home alone. But some how I knew something was different this night. That night morbid visions of mom being murdered and raped ran through this 9 year-olds imagination. That night my mom was with a group of people that turned her on to shooting cocaine intravenously, she took it in and went into convulsions, everyone left except for one junkie who went back and got her but by then it was to late.

My next memory is sitting in the other side of the room, as my mom whispered across the phone to my grandmother that she just found out she was HIV positive. She had contracted HIV that night. She did it one too many times that night, this time it ended up being more than just a high.

A few years later, during the 90's in Chicago, I made my best friends in my 7th grade class. My very best friend had an older brother involved in the hip hop and gang culture on the streets. At that time, I became engrafted into the Hip-Hop Culture. I began to drink heavily and to do graffiti. By the end of the year, I had become friends with a tougher and older crowd.

I began to hang out with them and they became my family. This family was what Time Magazine described as one of the nation's most notorious gangs.

With gang involvement came the drugs. Some on who I looked up to very much a respected writer in Chicago who also was a feared gang member in my neighborhood introduced me to drugs (even though my mom dealt I had never tried it). Now that I had begun to get high, my mother and I found we had something in common. We started getting high together, mom and her 12-year-old son. Soon she found someone to help her make drug transactions while she was out.

I began to get into the drug game myself and not only sold but had several working for me on the streets selling everything from weed to crack cocaine, PCP, LSD. Besides selling drugs I too became a heavy user. Often using up what I was suppose to sell. During this time, I was continually having trouble with the law. My criminal record had officially begun. A year later, I was not only a full-blown gangster, and made leader of the shorties (youth).

Shortly after at a nation wide meeting (which brought the heads together from all over) I was able to meet the leader of my entire organization. Immediately, I found favor in his eyes, which led me to get all the guns, drugs and support from other sections to start my own little section. Soon after I founded the set, the Chicago police brought me down. The Alderman of the ward had singled me out and had me harassed until I finally got arrested and thrown in jail.

I found myself in prison. I learned the ropes and became the leader of the crew for all Latin Folks with almost half of the deck in our club. In prison, kids were rapped, stabbed, beaten and taken advantage of yet my crew stuck together and fought when needed. Eventually the fighting climaxed into a riot in the prison gym.

Over 60 gang members fought, not only each other, but also against the security until they were able to get us all on lock down. Now I found myself in solitary confinement, all by myself, not counting the hundreds of roaches that crawled around the cell all night long.

One day, as I laid in confinement my aunt showed up with my uncle and my older sister. I thought they had come to visit. I thought it was going to be a good day, a relief from that dark dungeon, but instead it became the worst day of my life. When life could not dare deal another disastrous blow I was given the final assault. The tidings of bad news that came that day sucked out all the spirit I had left. Mom had died.

AIDS had accomplished its purpose and had defeated my mom's ability to fight off a common cold, which escalated into a deadly case of double pneumonia. Now how do I go back to my deck crying? I cannot show any weakness in the midst of my adversaries. Thank God, my worst enemies in prison were able to sympathize with the death of a mother. They came to my comfort.

I was quickly released to an uncle, by petition of my parole officer, who promised the judge I would now be reformed. Yet, weeks later I ended up back in jail. My probation officer pleaded with the courts to place me in drug rehab instead of downstate to D.O.C. It seemed as if God had given me another chance! I served 6 months in rehab where I began to awaken and realize I did not want to end up dead like my mother and father or back in jail. I made a decision to stay off drugs and away from the gangs.

Now my time in rehab was up, but they could not find a State transition home that would accept me because of the nature of my criminal record. They finally found a place 7 hours north of Chicago in Eau Claire, WI. I went there on the promise of a three-month stay till a place in Chicago was found for me. Those three months turned into over a year.

Although I seemed to be living this nightmare alone I soon found out I was not. One year had passed from when my mother called me on the phone telling me she only had 6 months to live. She never did make it those 6 months but that phone call, which came on Valentine's Day, was haunting me that Valentine's week of 1995.

However, around that time, God in His love sent a team of missionaries from Mexico to Eau Claire, WI. After watching their mime presentation of the Gospel, I tried to argue with them all that my dear grandmother had taught me about God from the Jehovah's Witness religion. To my disappointment, this Mexican team of ministers barely spoke English and couldn't debate with me. Nevertheless they kept on asking me "would you like to have God in your life? God loves you just like you are."

"Wow! Really? Well, who wouldn't want God" I responded. I'm just too bad. I am not ready to stop smoking, listening to worldly music and fooling around with the ladies. He brushed those comments off and told me not to let what God forgave me of keep me away from Christ. February 21st, 1996 I opened my heart to Christ with a man who did not even speak my language and I have never been the same since.

I was released to some older cousins of my mother in 1997, which had just been saved independently from my salvation experience around the same time. When we found out we were both newly saved they petitioned the State to get custody and I was released. That fall, I walked into my first

Christian Church and weeks later was water baptized, totally delivered from drug addiction and filled with the Holy Ghost with the evidence of speaking in other tongues. Immediately, God called me to the five-fold ministry.

CHAPTER 8

WHERE NO MAN HAS GONE BEFORE

"IF YOUR LIFE STYLE IS TOO COMFORTABLE IT'S A SIGN THAT YOU'RE NOT GIVING ENOUGH" CS LEWIS

In Mark chapter 16:15 Jesus gave some of his final words to his children and said go into the all the world and preach the gospel to every creature. Yet 2,000 years later Christians still only go to the evangelized to preach the gospel to non-practicing Christians in Christian nations.

Often times we champion mission campaigns where we have altar calls filled with culturally Christian people "getting saved," when actually it was really just Catholics being brought to an altar to become protestant, or better yet backsliders returning to a life of faith at best. Even worse is the millions spent on ministry in Christian nations to see people answer altar calls for fire insurance with no real conversion experience. Yet we call it brining the gospel to the lost.

2,000 years ago Christ came and died for the world, yet 2/3 of the planet is still classified as un-evangelized. Meaning never heard the gospel. The late great T.L. Osborne (Christian missionary to Africa) once said nobody should hear the gospel twice until everyone has heard it once.

Another on my hero's is the legendary China Inland Missions founder Hudson Taylor who once said "Given the command to go, we need not any special calling to go, but we must pray do I have a special calling to stay." If you do have that special calling to stay in the evangelized world, your duty still remains to obey Christ call in full filing the Great Commission. However your role in not going means that you are sowing to support those reaching the un-evangelized. The epidemic the church faces however is that most Christians don't tithe, and when they do tithe their churches are not reaching the un-evangelized with those resources, and the Christians feel like they have done their duty in giving to the Lord.

Barna Research discovered that churches in North America collectively spend more money on choir robe cleaning solution than on the un-evangelized nations. Then when churches do something it's usually in South or Central America (Catholic people) or Africa and Haiti. Figuratively bringing water to the ocean. Pastors and churches have yet to grasp the command in the Holy

Scriptures given by the Apostle Paul to aim where Christ has NOT been named.

Romans 15:20

...preach the gospel, not where Christ was named, lest I should build upon another man's foundation"

Yet for those dear saints who are only to steward their personal giving to the Lord and feel you have done so by supporting your local Church, I leave you with this challenging thought by C.S. Lewis in his classic disposition on the Christian faith, Mere Christianity "if your life style is too comfortable it's a sign that you're not giving enough." Let's do a little extra and support ministries like ours reaching non-Christian nations under heavy persecution so that together so that "the Lamb who was slain would receive the reward of His suffering." *Moravian missionaries Johann Leonhard Dober and David Nitschmann*

If you like to be a part of the harvest here in South East Asia you may do so by giving online at

www.AnifBeijing.com/give

Chapter 9

Prayers & Confessions

Prayer of Salvation

If you read this book but you didn't consider yourself born again yet, then you are in great danger.

Tomorrow is not promised to any man. Therefore you must make a decision today to follow God, and repent of your sins.

There is nothing standing in the way any more between you and God, because Christ nailed your sin to the cross in His own body.

All you have to do is repent, confess your sin and believe on the Lord Jesus

Christ with me now, and you will be saved.

Just pray this prayer with me and make this decision now. You will never regret it!

"Father God, I come to you now, just as I am. I ask you to forgive me of my sins, and come into my heart. I believe that your son Jesus Christ died for my sins and on the third day he was raised from the dead.

From this day forward I belong to you. In Jesus name, Amen"

If you have prayed that prayer and believe in your heart, you shall be saved. Now just follow the next steps given to you in this book and you will enter a glorious destiny!

Before He formed you in the womb He knew you and had a plan for your life.

Follow steps 1, 2, 3, and 4 as laid out in this book and you will be well on your way to healthy vibrant and glorious new life in Christ.

You need to get your own copy of The Holy Bible.

I put in a few books of the Bible in here now to get you started till you get your own.

Confess these 15 verses from the Bible aloud every day for the next few months and practice your personal prayer tongue each day for 30 minutes a day minimum.

CONFESSIONS

Who/What I Am in Christ

- I am reigning in life by Jesus Christ (Romans 5:17)

- I am not looking at the things that are seen, but at the things which are not seen (II Corinthians 4:18)

- I am walking by faith and not by sight (II Corinthians 5:7)

- I am casting down imaginations and every high thing that exalts itself against the knowledge of God (II Corinthians 10:5)

- I am the righteousness of God in Christ Jesus (II Corinthians 5:21)

- I am rooted and grounded in love, because Christ dwells within me (Ephesians 3:17)

- I am the workmanship of God, created in Christ Jesus for good works (Ephesians 2:10)

- I am a partaker of God's divine nature (II Peter 1:4)

- I am prosperous and in good health, because my soul prospers (III John 2)

- I am being transformed by the renewing of my mind to prove the perfect will of God (Romans 12:2)

- I am healed by the stripes of Jesus Christ (1 Peter 2:24)

- I am more than a conqueror through Jesus Christ (Romans 8:37)

- I am the salt of the earth, and the light of the world (Matthew 5:13a, 14a)

- I am complete in Christ (Colossians 2:10)

- I am strong in the Lord and in the power of His might (Ephesians 6:10)

- I am taking the shield of faith and quenching all of the fiery darts of the enemy (Ephesians 6:16)

- I am praying my desires and receiving them (Mark 11:24)

- I am like a tree planted by the rivers of water and everything that I do prospers (Psalm 1:3)

- I am a temple of the Holy Ghost (I Corinthians 6:19)

- I am given exceeding great and precious promises, and by them

I partake of the divine nature,
having escaped the corruption
that is in the world through lust
(II Peter 1:4)

- I am led by the spirit of God;
  therefore, I am a son of God
  (Romans 8:14)

- I am not walking after the flesh,
  but after the Spirit (Romans 8:1)

- I am receiving all of my needs
  met according to His riches in
  glory by Christ Jesus (Philippians
  4:19)

- I am casting all of my cares upon
  Him, because I know He cares
  for me (I Peter 5:7)

- I am blessed with all spiritual
  blessings in Christ Jesus
  (Ephesians 1:3)

- I am blessed when I come in, and blessed when I go out (Deuteronomy 28:6)

- I am an heir of God and a joint-heir with Jesus Christ (Romans 8:17)

- I am increasing and abounding in love (I Thessalonians 3:12)

- I am being made perfect in every good work to do God's will (Hebrews 13:21)

- I am showing forth the praise of God (Psalms 51:15)

Biography

I was called into the ministry in the fall of 1997 at just 18 years old. At that time God said, "Evangelist, Evangelist, Evangelist" and not knowing what that meant I joined the street witnessing team at Dr. Bill Winston's Church in Forest Park, Illinois "Living Word Christian Center," serving as an street Evangelist. He didn't think I could be an official minister of the gospel since I was an orphan, former gang member and recovering drug addict

But later in 2002 Dr. Winston sent him to Rod Parsley's World Harvest Church in Columbus, Ohio where I graduated Manga Cum Lade in Cross Cultural Ministries, and was ordained on July 16th, 2005. From 2005 I have served 4 assistant pastor positions in Delaware, Chicago, Montreal and till my current role as Senior Pastor of All Nations

International Fellowship in South East Asia. I have the privilege to minister in over14 nations of the world, seeing miracles, healing, salvation and corporate outpourings of the Holy Spirit in signs, wonders and manifestations.

Married to Jade Wang of Heilongjiang province in China, since 2010. I now balance my ministry with business, and secular media career in China, while raising our two young sons.

I have led a campaign to heal the wounds of colonialism between Africa and the nations involved with the scramble for Africa to foster spiritual catharsis. As a strong supporter of Israel, I hosted a large-scale event to educate the public on the dangers of anti-Semitism and other racial prejudices.

Media is another major area of my ministry to impact Asia. I have been featured
in various Chinese international newspapers dozens of times, including "China Daily," Global Times, Hong Kong's "China Southern Morning Post" and has been featured on China's international radio CRI show "Expat Tales," Tencent News, Xinhua news, CNTV, and many other media outlets in regards to business as the founder of Nations Abroad Consulting Ltd, or as a social commentary and religious leader.

My impact is on a national scale via the multiple appearances via Beijing TV, CCTV 3, CCTV 4, Tianjin TV, hosting and co hosting shows, I have become a national celebrity and a household name throughout the country. Sharing my life's experience, strength, and hope.

My vision remains to reach non-evangelized people groups in Laos, Vietnam, Mongolia, Cambodia, Indonesia, Malaysia, and China.

I've had the honor to preach, teach, or share throughout North America and Europe including but not limited to:

- Rhema Bible Training Center Tula, Oklahoma

- Oral Roberts University, Tulsa Oklahoma

- Victory Bible College Tulsa, Oklahoma

- World Harvest Church Columbus, Ohio "Rod Parsley"

- Living Word Christian Center Forest Park, Illinois "Dr. Bill Winston"

As well as many lesser known churches worldwide. Since 2016 my Church All Nations International Fellowship has began launching Miracle & Healing Crusades around Asia Pacific and have already ministered in five crusades, four in Philippines, with the first being in Mongolia with over 2,500 in attendance accompanied by notable healings, miracles, signs and wonders. More video footage and photos can be found on Facebook public profile page Joseph Ricardo Castillo or on his Church's AllNationsInterntionalFell owship or ANIF's YouTube channel "Anif Church." To listen to weekly messages for free subscribe to Joseph Castillo on your podcast player or direct online at www.Anif.Buzzsprout.com